D0484901

Short Morning Prayers

Blue Mountain Arts®

New and Best-Selling Titles

By Susan Polis Schutz:
To My Daughter with Love on the Important Things in Life
To My Grandchild with Love
To My Son with Love

By Douglas Pagels:
Always Remember How Special You Are to Me
Required Reading for All Teenagers
The Next Chapter of Your Life
You Are One Amazing Lady

By Marci:
Angels Are Everywhere!
Friends Are Forever
10 Simple Things to Remember
To My Daughter
To My Granddaughter
To My Mother
To My Son
You Are My "Once in a Lifetime"

By Wally Amos, with Stu Glauberman:
The Path to Success Is Paved with Positive Thinking

By Minx Boren:
Friendship Is a Journey
Healing Is a Journey

By Carol Wiseman:
Emerging from the Heartache of Loss

Anthologies:
A Daybook of Positive Thinking
A Son Is Life's Greatest Gift
Dream Big, Stay Positive, and Believe in Yourself
Girlfriends Are the Best Friends of All
God Is Always Watching Over You
The Love Between a Mother and Daughter Is Forever
Nothing Fills the Heart with Joy like a Grandson
There Is Nothing Sweeter in Life Than a Granddaughter
There Is So Much to Love About You… Daughter
Think Positive Thoughts Every Day
Words Every Woman Should Remember
You Are Stronger Than You Know

Short Morning Prayers

A Collection
of Heartfelt Prayers
to Start Your Day

Debra DiPietro

Blue Mountain Press™
Boulder, Colorado

Copyright © 2017 by Debra DiPietro.
Copyright © 2017 by Blue Mountain Arts, Inc.

All rights reserved. No part of this publication may be reproduced, stored in a retrieval system or transmitted in any form or by any means, electronic, mechanical, photocopying, recording or otherwise, without the written permission of the publisher.

Library of Congress Control Number: 2016959027
ISBN: 978-1-68088-127-1

▌and Blue Mountain Press are registered in U.S. Patent and Trademark Office.
Certain trademarks are used under license.

Printed in China.
Fifth printing: 2021

♻ This book is printed on recycled paper.

This book is printed on paper that has been specially produced to be acid free (neutral pH) and contains no groundwood or unbleached pulp. It conforms with the requirements of the American National Standards Institute, Inc., so as to ensure that this book will last and be enjoyed by future generations.

Blue Mountain Arts, Inc.

P.O. Box 4549, Boulder, Colorado 80306

In the early morning light,
in the quiet of the dawn...
all things feel possible.
Thank you for this new day and
the clean slate it represents.
When things become busier later on,
this time, place, and peaceful space
will still reside within,
providing energy, strength,
clarity, guidance, and love
all day long.

Introduction

How we spend our first few minutes after waking up can greatly affect the rest of our day. Being still and quiet in the morning makes it easier to be focused, centered, and productive all day long. I personally use this time to get in touch with God and connect to my higher power. By doing this, I know it is going to be a great day.

I keep a few spiritual books and my writing journal on my nightstand. Some mornings, after reading a few passages, I am inspired to write a prayer, a poem, or a few thoughts for my new day. What you have in your hands is a collection of prayers that I have written in my personal journal or on my blog, *The Warm Milk Journal.* When I shared my first morning prayer on my blog back in March 2011, I never expected such a positive response. Today, "A Short Morning Prayer for a New Day" continues to be my most popular post. It is the first prayer you'll read in this book, and it was the inspiration for all that follow.

Because life is dynamic and we don't always feel the same way on any given day, this book is composed of a variety of prayers to suit your different moods and circumstances.

There are entries for when you are feeling thankful and excited, as well as for when you are feeling scared, sad, or confused. There are prayers that affirm the good things you are currently experiencing or want more of and prayers that simply ask questions or solicit guidance. Finally, some are left for you to fill in the blanks with whatever inspires you. All these prayers are intentionally simple and short so that in only a minute or two your day may be uplifted.

This collection is not in any particular order. You are welcome to start at the beginning and read a prayer a day, or you could actively seek out one that resonates with you on a particular morning. You might also wish to skip around and select an entry to read at random. I should mention that I speak to God in these prayers, but please insert *Father, Universe, Mother Earth,* or whatever has meaning for you when you get in touch with the divine. My hope is you will enjoy these short morning prayers, no matter your beliefs or religious background.

May your day be blessed.

In peace,
Debra DiPietro

A Short Morning Prayer
for a New Day

Dear God,

I welcome the new day.

May I not rush around so much that I miss the beauty that is all around me.

May I thank one person today.

May I smile more than I frown.

May I think more loving thoughts than self-defeating ones.

Thank you for this day!

Amen.

How Can I Be of Service Today?

Dear God,

I simply wish to ask you this morning, "How can I be of service?"

As I sit here with you in silence, a few ideas come to mind:

I can talk less and listen more.

I can slow down on the roads today and look for ways to be more considerate of my fellow travelers.

I can smile.

I can ask others, "How are you doing?" and really mean it and take an interest in them.

Thank you for your guidance. I look forward to this day so much.

Amen.

Keeping the Morning Alive
Throughout the Day

Dear God,

In the early morning light,
in the quiet of the dawn…
all things feel possible!

I am fresh and filled with
an abundance of gratitude.

As the day turns to night,
may I not become too weary.
I pray I remain thankful
and aware of the possibilities,
which exist so long as I continue
to see them.

Amen.

Marveling in Awe

Dear God,

This is such a beautiful morning. How may I continue to marvel in awe of this day? I want to stay focused on my blessings, be as loving as I can be, and do my best.

If I stumble or get busy or lost, please gently put me back on the right path. I so want to enjoy this day full of promise.

I thank you, God, for hanging in there with me. I love you.

Amen.

A Monday Morning Prayer

Dear God,

As I begin this new week, I wish to thank you for all my present blessings. I pray that this week will be filled with meaningful work, creativity, and vibrant energy and that I will be able to see the best in challenges that come my way.

May I be up to whatever tasks are set before me.

Amen.

Prioritizing

Dear God,

Good morning! What do you have in store for me today? There is much that I wish to do at work and for my family and others.

Please help me to prioritize the one or two most important things today. If it doesn't all get done, may I be okay with that and let it go.

Amen.

Life and Opportunity

Dear God,

I am thankful for so many things right now. I thank you for my life and for every opportunity I have to tell someone special "I love you."

Amen.

Working to My Strengths

Dear God,

I am a little tired today. Please help me to focus on the things that energize me. I wish to remember to work to my strengths, ask for help when I need it, and not try to please everybody.

May I please you by taking care of myself and having a great day!

Amen.

A Question for the Day

Dear God,

Good morning! May I handle any challenges that come my way confidently. I have faith that I am where I need to be and doing what I need to be doing.

My question for the day is:

_____?

I appreciate your love and guidance.

Amen.

A Heart That Knows

Dear God,

Thank you for giving me a heart that knows how to love.

Thank you for surrounding me with loving and supportive people.

I never need to feel alone.

Amen.

Stretching Myself

Dear God,

As sleepiness lifts, I am aware
of this beautiful new day.

Please help me to
stretch myself at least once,
speed up when necessary,
slow down periodically,
and know which tasks need
my attention the most.

God, I have a lot on my plate
right now,
and I welcome your guidance.

Amen.

In Need of a Gentle Nudge

Dear God,

Please nudge me gently today.

I need some loving guidance to help me
be easy on myself and
do what I can with this day, but then
give myself permission to
let go of the rest by evening.

I thank you in advance.

Amen.

A Good Night's Sleep

Dear God,

Thank you for blessing me with a good night's sleep,
a fresh mind, and creative energy.

May I put this energy to good use by expressing
thanks more often than complaining and by
connecting with, loving, and helping others.

Amen.

Peace and Understanding

Dear God,

I pray for light and love for those in darkness, for those in pain, for those who are grieving. I pray for understanding among groups and cultures on our planet.

I pray for peace.

Amen.

Seeing the Beauty in Others

Dear God,

Thank you for my friends, family, colleagues, neighbors, and anyone else I may interact with today. Help me to see the beauty in all the people I encounter.

I do believe that, overall, people are good. We are all in this together. We are doing our best. I will try to keep this in mind and always be kind.

Amen.

Delightful Summer

Dear God,

How may I best spend these extra hours of light?

The sounds of children playing outside remind me that this is a good season to take a break and remember to play.

The heat of the day also nudges me to perhaps slow down a bit. Why be in such a hurry all the time?

During these dog days of summer, may I spend some carefree time enjoying leisurely activities such

as _____, _____,

and _____.

Thank you for this time to dream and bask in the sun and the simple pleasures of life.

Amen.

Am I Doing Enough?

Dear God,

I know I am far from perfect,
and sometimes I wonder if I am doing enough
to make a meaningful difference.
It is easy to get caught up
in the busyness and responsibilities of life
and forget the details that really matter.

Is what I am doing enough?
Will it pass the test of time?

Am I putting smiles on people's faces?
Am I circulating good in this world
through my thoughts, intentions, and actions?

Today I will work on these important things.
I will do my best
during my own humble life.

Amen.

Out of Sorts

Dear God,

Please forgive me on the days when I am feeling a little grumpy, impatient, and out of sorts. Even on those days, God, I am well-intentioned. Sometimes, however, I am just a bit off. Those are probably the days I need you most.

Thank you for your constant presence, guidance, and love, and for helping me return to the path of peace. I love you.

Amen.

Optimism

Dear God,

What a beautiful morning! May I go about this day with purpose and an optimistic spirit. I do not own any "problems." I will see the good and overcome any challenges that are put in my path.

Amen.

Being Open to New Things

Dear God,

I wish to please you today by
slowing down enough to notice
the beauty around me,
being the most loving I can be,
focusing on my life's purpose—
I know you know what it is—and
being open to new things.

Thank you, God, for listening
and for being there.

Amen.

Quiet and Loved

Dear God,

I appreciate this chance to be quiet and start off my
day with your love. I am grateful for this new day. I
have my health, and I feel well rested. May this day
be filled with blessings for myself and others.

Amen.

My Dreams and Inspirations

Dear God,

I feel stronger knowing you are at my side. I am grateful for this new day. I woke up with ideas about how I am going to make my dreams come true.

Here are a few inspirations I would like to share with you:

1. _____

2. _____

3. _____

Thank you for being my partner in life. It is all so very good!

Amen.

Something Unexpected

Dear God,

I am excited about this new day and what may happen. I will be enthusiastic as I go about my business.

May I see something unexpected, something that makes me laugh, and something that challenges me. I am excited about learning and growing. I thank you for all the opportunities that cross my path.

Amen.

Bigger Than My Problems

Dear God,

I am sleepy and not sure about today. Please help me to see the good that will inevitably happen, despite any challenges I may have to deal with. When the challenges do come, please help me to be strong and victorious.

I know that my faith in *you* is bigger than any perceived problems.

Amen.

Under My Control or Not

Dear God,

May I do my best with the things that are under my control today. May I take action where appropriate, see the opportunities and the good around me, inspire others, and do what I can to be productive.

May I not stress about the things that are not under my influence, such as the weather or other people's decisions and behavior. Please help me to accept and release what I can't control.

Thank you.

Amen.

By My Side

Dear God,

When I am feeling under the weather,
you are by my side.

When I am in the mood to celebrate,
you are by my side.

When I feel doubt,
you are by my side.

As I go about the tasks of my daily life,
you are by my side.

I am ever thankful,
for you are by my side.

Amen.

So Many Blessings

Good morning, God!

I feel so blessed in many ways. I am loved. I am safe. I am secure.

I thank you for looking over me and keeping me and my family safe as we slept last night.

I thank you for the comfort of my bed and the roof over my head.

For these blessings, I am thankful.

Amen.

The Things I Love

Dear God,

I am so grateful for this new day. May I spend it doing work I love, helping the community I love, and spending time with people I love.

Amen.

May the Smallest Boat Rise with the Largest Ship

Dear God,

Please guide me on this day, for there are challenges in my life and our world right now.

Please help me to always choose love over anything else.

May I practice forgiveness and acceptance rather than fall into resentment and judgment.

May all our children out there be well fed and cared for.

May we all do our part to help each other to bring out the best we have to offer. In that way, the smallest boat will rise with the largest ship, and we will all be lifted up.

Amen.

Quieting My Mind

Dear God,

Please help me to be a better listener. Help me to know it is a good thing to be quiet and still. I can unplug. I don't have to check e-mail or social media every few minutes. Please help me to relax and quiet my mind throughout the day.

Amen.

When Times Are Good

Dear God,

Thank you for all the times I feel vibrant.

Maybe I don't thank you enough when times are good, so I am thanking you right now.

Amen.

More to Be Thankful For

Dear God,

It seems the more I give thanks, the more I have in my life to feel thankful for.

This morning, I am thankful for:

1. _____

2. _____

3. _____

4. _____

5. _____

I am so grateful to you for all my blessings.

Amen.

Under the Weather

Dear God,

Sometimes when I am not feeling my best, I get down.
During these times, help me to remember that soon I will be
feeling like myself again.

I will make a conscious effort to keep my spirits up.

I pray for all those in need of healing right now. They have
my love, and I see them as healthy and whole.

Amen.

Staying the Course

Dear God,

Am I on a good path? Sometimes I stray and get a little lost,
but I know my faith and my internal compass will always
bring me back to you and the right path.

Amen.

Curve Balls

Dear God,

Please give me strength when I am challenged by a person or situation in my life. It is not always easy to stay centered and calm when something hits unexpectedly. Please help me to react peacefully to life's curve balls.

Thank you.

Amen.

Finding My Patience

Dear God,

I am in need of some patience today. I find when I am busy I forget to stop and take a breath.

May I find time to reflect and be still. May I think loving thoughts about myself and others.

Amen.

A Fall Prayer

Dear God,

Thank you for this fall day.
The season is newly changing.
The cooler air brings a fresh new energy.
I appreciate this time of the year that serves to
remind us to pause from all our busy doings
and perhaps slow down a bit.

I am thankful for many things.
I can see beauty and impermanence all around me.
This combination leaves me with bittersweet feelings
of awe, humility, and gratitude.

God, with your help, may I never take
this precious gift of life for granted.

Amen.

Forgiving Myself

Dear God,

I realize there are things that I haven't completely forgiven myself for yet. There were times when I spoke unkind words that I will never be able to take back. I may have taken an easier path when I could have challenged myself more.

Here is something I don't feel proud of:

_____.

Please help me to let this go and forgive myself. I am not perfect. If I hurt someone else, may they find it within themselves to forgive me as I am working now to forgive myself.

As I toil with this, God, I thank you for always forgiving me no matter what. At the end of the day, may I learn from your unconditional love and wisdom.

Forgiveness equals peace. What a wonderful lesson.

Thank you.

Amen.

At an Impasse

Dear God,

This morning, please help me to find peace despite any conflict in my life. When an impasse occurs, help me to handle it with grace and dignity. When I have a disagreement with someone, help me to remember that the world does not necessarily revolve around me and not everyone is always going to see things my way.

May a resolution arise, but even if one does not, may I find peace despite this impasse. With your help, may I find the strength to let go of the need to be "right."

Each time I consider another's point of view, my world and life experience expand.

Amen.

Celebrating

Dear God,

I feel like celebrating this new day! With a joyful heart, I thank you for this morning. I will set about my business with a spring in my step. I have important work to do.

I am especially grateful for _____.

Three things that fill my heart with joy are:

1._____

2._____

3._____

Amen.

Feeling Thankful

Dear God,

From the moment I first get out of bed this morning to the time I turn the lights out to retire tonight, I will feel thankful.

I am healthy. I am loved. I am focused. I am at peace.

Amen.

Lightening Up

Dear God,

Sometimes I find myself worrying endlessly. I worry about making mistakes and not achieving the life I am supposed to be living. I put pressure on myself, and as a result, I get so tired.

Please help me to lighten up and permit myself times of joy and frivolity. Work is important, but so are play and time to just do nothing.

Amen.

Glad to Be a Part of It

Dear God,

What an amazing world we have. I am so happy to be a part of it. Today I intend to hug my loved ones more and dance whenever I feel like it.

Thank you for your love. Thank you for my life.

Amen.

Another Chance

Dear God,

Thank you for another day. I have been given another chance to get some things right, such as complaining less and doing all that I can to make the lives of the people around me a little brighter.

Thank you for this opportunity.

Amen.

A Fresh Perspective

Dear God,

Please help me see things with a fresh perspective today.

When someone is talking to me, may I really listen to them.

If someone needs my help, may I say yes.

May words of encouragement come out of my mouth, and may love be my guide.

Please help me to do all these things.

Amen.

All About Love

Dear God,

All I wish to do this morning is focus on *love*: your love, the love that is all around me. I am at peace when I know that I am loved and that I *am* love.

Amen.

At Home in Nature

Dear God,

When I hear the sounds of nature,
I feel so close to you.
Crickets and frogs harmonizing at dusk
inspire me to sing and rejoice.
When I feel the wind
and hear the rustling of the trees,
I smile and stretch to embrace the natural world
because deep down I know I am a part of it.
When I desire respite from my responsibilities,
I simply need to take a step outside.
Within minutes of basking in your greenery
underneath the open sky,
my soul is replenished and at peace.

Thank you for the beautiful world you created
that I am lucky enough to call home.

Amen.

How Can I Best Use This Day?

Dear God,

How can I best use this day? I am setting an intention to make the most of this day for my good and the greater good of all. Please assist me with this intention.

Thank you.

Amen.

I Feel Encouraged Today

Dear God,

As the sunlight filters through the clouds, I feel encouraged that today is going to be a great day. I hope to make someone laugh, complete a project that needs tending to, and give myself time to be still and connect with you.

Amen.

Tending to the Things That Matter

Dear God,

Please help me to be present, to let go of the things that don't really matter, and to tend to the things that do.

Will it matter if I make someone smile today?

Will it matter if I stop rushing around so much?

Will it matter if I stay focused on being my most loving self?

I think I know the answers to these questions, God.

Amen.

I Don't Wish to Whine

Dear God,

I am not here to complain. I don't wish to whine. I appreciate the blessings that are already in my life. I trust you have a plan for me that is better than I can imagine. I have fun imagining the possibilities though, God. I really do.

Thank you for giving me a sound and creative mind. I am using it to create the best life possible for myself and those around me.

Amen.

Daily News

Dear God,

Please help me when I sometimes doubt myself, worry, or take the daily news too seriously. I know all is well, and I am strong in my faith. Thank you for being there whenever I wobble just a tiny bit.

Amen.

Thank You for Helping Me

Dear God,

Thank you for this day. I feel blessed to sit comfortably in my cozy home, surrounded by those I love.

On this day, please help me to see the good in people's hearts and actions and in the natural beauty right in my own backyard.

Thank you for helping me to grow. Thank you for helping me to learn. Thank you for helping me build my courage and find and use my voice.

This is a wonderful time in my life, and I am blessed!

Amen.

Health and Healing

Dear God,

Thank you for answering my prayers. I enjoy good health, and those around me are happy and healthy too. If somebody I care about is suffering in any way, I pray and affirm their wellness and wholeness.

Amen.

Take the Wheel

Dear God,

I turn this day over to you. I am choosing to let go. I let go of worries, expectations, and judgments. Thank you for taking over the steering wheel and letting me be the passenger. I trust you have put me on the road I am supposed to travel today.

Amen.

Overwhelmed

Dear God,

I sometimes feel a little overwhelmed by life. When I do, I am grateful to you for being there. Help me remember to stop and take a breath.

I pray for guidance and clarity.

The important things for me to focus on today are:

1. _____

2. _____

3. _____

Thank you.

Amen.

Finding Light in Winter

Dear God,

The days are short and nights are long.

I have more time to reflect and pray.

Taking stock of this past year, what went well? Is there anything I fear? Are there shadows lurking inside me?

Even though there may be darkness outside my window right now, I will seek out light in other ways. A lit candle, holiday lights, the sparkling stars and moon at night… all are reminders of your love and the miracle that is my life.

Spring will come soon enough, and the light will return. It always does.

I thank you for this time to nest and turn inward.

Amen.

A Go-Giver

Dear God,

How can I be a go-giver rather than a go-getter?
I have spent so much of my life worrying about
myself. Now I am thinking it should be the other
way around—that I should focus my attention on
helping others. How can I give more and make the
lives around me better?

Amen.

Children

Dear God,

Thank you for watching over our community's
children. May they be loved and cared for. May they
never know hunger or shame.

Amen.

Shelter

Dear God,

I feel safe, dry, and protected. Modern-day inventions such as air conditioning and heating keep me comfortable no matter the time of year. I have a roof over my head. Clothes cover me and help me project who I wish to be out in the world. At home, what I wear helps me to feel comfortable and snug. I also think of the protection of your love that keeps me afloat when times are challenging.

Shelter keeps us cozy and keeps us from being exposed. I would like to say a special prayer to anyone in the community or the world who does not have this basic human comfort. I send love and warmth to people without a home or who are displaced from their homes due to weather, war, or poverty. If there is anybody out there feeling alone, may they feel loved and supported. If there is anybody out there cold or hungry, may they be fed and warm and cared for.

Amen.

A Gift of Solitude

Dear God,

I welcome this gift of a few minutes of solitude and quiet. Before the busyness of my day begins, I wish to thank you for my health, my family, and my home.

Please help me to see the good in everybody I meet today.

Amen.

Nurturing My Spirit

Dear God,

May I remember to take care of the things that nurture my spirit today. Perhaps that will mean spending time outdoors, sharing a meal with people I love, and having a little quiet time with you.

Amen.

If I Get Grumpy...

Dear God,

Please help me to stay centered and peaceful throughout the day and to keep my priorities straight. When I feel stressed, please help me remember to breathe deeply and fully and to let out any tension.

If I get grumpy, gently remind me of what a gift today is.

Thank you for everything that I have.

Amen.

Paying It Forward

Dear God,

Thank you for this beautiful morning. I am grateful to have this new day. How may I pay it forward today?

I can give some time and lend a hand to a neighbor, colleague, or community organization. I can leave a small anonymous gift, such as flowers, on another's porch or pay for a fellow patron's coffee or meal.

Yes, God, this day is full of possibility.

Amen.

Challenges

Dear God,

Thank you for the challenges that make me grow. Even if I struggle at first, I end up feeling more confident when I overcome them. Please help me remember this when the next challenge comes along.

Please help me to be brave when I feel scared, to be strong when I feel weak, and to always keep things in perspective.

Amen.

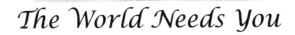

The World Needs You

Dear God,

There are many concerns weighing on the world right now. I pray for good leadership in our communities and countries of the world so that we can all prosper, feel safe, and be responsible stewards of our planet for our children and their children.

God, I wish for our leaders to have these qualities:

_____, _____, and

_____.

I hope that all people around the world, including

myself, work on _____.

A community is only as good as its citizens and leadership. Please look after us. We need you now more than ever.

Amen.

Clean Slate

Dear God,

In the stillness, I know all things are possible. Thank you for this new day and the clean slate that it represents. Please help me to make the most of it by slowing down, appreciating the kindness of others, and believing in myself.

Thank you.

Amen.

A Peaceful Space

Dear God,

Thank you for this time. It is quiet. It is still. I am at peace. When the day gets busier later on, I will remember this time, place, and peaceful space.

Amen.

Tough Choices

Dear God,

On this morning, I reflect on choices I have made in my life. I so wish not to have any regrets. Who is to say if a decision made was a good one or not? Perhaps the best choice is to let go of judgment.

God, today please help me remember that there are no bad decisions. At the time I made a decision, I was doing my best with what information I had. I can always learn and move on. I don't need to hold on to anything. I do not need to judge or feel regret.

Thank you for your unconditional love, acceptance, and guidance.

Amen.

Tuning Out the Noise

Dear God,

No matter what the news anchors are talking about on the television or what I may see on the Internet, I can choose peace.

I can allow peace to come into my heart by:

_____.

The world is beautiful. What I think about becomes my reality. May I tune out the noise today and focus on your love.

Amen.

Procrastination

Dear God,

Good morning! I sometimes struggle with my priorities, and I know I procrastinate when I should be getting things done.

Please help me to concentrate today on what needs to be taken care of.

Amen.

Little Things

Dear God,

Thank you for the "little things" that make life so wonderful: an unexpected smile from a stranger, hugs and encouragement from colleagues, friends, and loved ones, a kind word here and there.

These little things mean so much. I will focus on these wonderful blessings today.

Thank you.

Amen.

Thinking of You

Dear God,

When I take my first few breaths today, I will think of you. As I take my first few steps today, I will think of you. Walking and breathing immersed in love, I am whole. I am peace.

Amen.

Living in the Present

Dear God,

I am doing my best to forgive the past and live in the present. I appreciate the little (and sometimes big) reminders that are put in my path each day to enjoy and appreciate the life I have *now*.

Amen.

Taking the High Road

Dear God,

Today I wish to soar above any difficulties and take the higher road. If a person or circumstance threatens to upset my center, I know I can stay on my path and not get hijacked.

Thank you, God, for peace.

Thank you, God, for strength.

Thank you, God, for this moment.

It will be a great day!

Amen.

Adventures

Dear God,

I am excited about this day and the adventures in store for me. May I keep my mind, heart, and spirit open to whatever develops. I would love to try something new today. Whatever will it be?

Amen.

Being Pain-Free

Dear God,

Thank you for this new day. I appreciate feeling refreshed and pain-free.

For those in pain, for those who have loved ones in pain, for people who have lost someone they love: I pray for them so they know they are loved and not alone.

Amen.

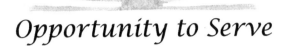

Opportunity to Serve

Dear God,

I am so grateful for the opportunity to serve.
These are the people I would like to serve today:

_____, _____,

and _____.

I am full of joy at the thought of all the meaningful
work I am going to do today.

When my work is done, I will rest and enjoy some
quiet time with you. I know that as I go about my
day, you are at my side. I thank you. I love you.

Amen.

A Spring Prayer

Dear God,

As the tulips pierce through the snow, I know
spring is around the corner.

As the light returns and my garden flushes
with its first round of color,
I wish to give thanks.

I thank you for every time in my life that
I get to start again.

It is a gift to start each day anew.

May this season of new life inspire me
to grow and renew a sense of purpose and love.

I am light, and the heaviness of winter is lifting.

Amen.

A New Beginning

Dear God,

I will play at making this day a blessing by finding the lightness in all things and people.

I will seek the love and joy that is sometimes hidden behind dark and heavy moods and tasks.

Oh, to release the fun energy in the middle of the workday—now *that* is an accomplishment worthy of my attention.

Thank you, thank you, thank you for this new day of life.

I will create a new beginning starting now.

Amen.

Being Mindful

Dear God,

May I finish things I've started, move on from the things that are already finished or no longer need my attention, and be mindful of what really matters to me.

I am excited about serving others and learning new things.

Amen.

Looking for the Sunshine

Dear God,

As I go about my day today, I will look for the sunshine, the open doors, and the smiles.

I pray for the folks who are not smiling today. Please help me to come from a loving place and pure heart when interacting with these people.

Amen.

One Good Deed

Dear God,

What kind of day do you have in store for me? I hope that I can contribute something positive to the world around me today. Help me to do at least one good deed to help another today.

With that deed done, someone's burdens may be lifted a bit, and I may end this day with a lighter step and a heart filled with compassion.

I feel loved, and I know I am being taken care of. I will make an effort today to help others feel loved and taken care of too.

Amen.

Clarity on Purpose

Dear God,

At times I feel so small in this big world. There are many challenges in today's society. If I wanted to help, where would I even begin? Perhaps I can start with you. I will start this morning in silence and ask a few questions, and then listen.

Some questions I have are:

What difference can I make?

What is the best work I can do right now?

When it all feels overwhelming, I pray that I will find peace, solace, and purpose.

I thank you for this clarity and guidance.

Amen.

Cooling My Anger

Dear God,

Sometimes I can get stuck in anger and feel like a volcano that may erupt at any time. This is very draining and toxic. When I feel wronged by the actions of another person or some set of circumstances that did not match my original expectations, may I choose peace instead of anger. May I gracefully let go of whatever is bothering me.

Over time, anger turns into resentment and, like the lava from a volcano, can burn anything it touches. Smoldering anger will eventually give in to explosive outbursts that can do myself and those I love harm.

I know there is another way. Molten rock in the earth's heart can be released peacefully and flow into the ocean where it steams upon entry and then quietly dissipates.

I will breathe and work on cooling that heat of anger inside me. May it subside and leave my heart and body.

Amen.

Keeping Life Interesting

Dear God,

Thank you for giving me enough challenges to keep life interesting and to keep me from getting lazy or taking things for granted.

I will do my best today. May I practice patience and forgiveness.

Amen.

Peace

Dear God,

This morning I pray for peace. For those in conflict, for those in mourning, for those who feel lost at the moment… may there be peace.

Amen.

Life Is Good

Dear God,

When all is said and done, life is pretty good. What do I have to complain about? Throughout this day, I will make an effort to really see and experience the blessings that are all around me. When I stray, I know you will nudge me lovingly and before I know it I will be back on track.

I know this day will be an amazing one. I am ready.

Amen.

Walking with Confidence

Dear God,

I am strong and self-assured. I will walk confidently and go about my day knowing I have you at my side. Thank you for your love. Thank you for believing in me. I love you.

Amen.

People I've Lost Touch With

Dear God,

There are people who once were very important to me that I have lost touch with. There are many reasons for this. We may no longer live near each other, our lives may have taken different directions, or we may just be too caught up in the busyness of life to nurture the relationship.

For those people I want to keep in my life, may I find a way to make the time to reconnect. Perhaps a phone call, a lunch date, or an old-fashioned letter is in order.

As for the rest… my old loves and friends or colleagues who are no longer in my life: I wish them well and send them my love. I am richer because of the time we spent together.

Amen.

Saying Goodbye

Dear God,

At times it is hard to let go of people, memories, jobs, and other life circumstances. Please help me let go and say goodbye to them when it is time to do so.

Amen.

A Fresh Start

Dear God,

I know that each morning I have an opportunity to transition to something new. I have a fresh start and that is today. Right now.

What is possible? Anything!

Amen.

Confident or Unsure

Dear God,

There are mornings when I feel confident and times when I feel unsure of myself. Please gently guide me to see all the virtue and potential that is in me and all the important work you have for me to do today.

Thank you so much.

Amen.

Rising Above

Dear God,

How may I soar above my challenges and petty (or big) concerns of the day? God, sometimes I get tired or overwhelmed, and I am not sure what to do. Please give me the energy, strength, and clarity to give my all today.

I wish a good day for all those around me and in other parts of the world who I know have even greater challenges than my own.

Amen.

A Lighthearted Day

Dear God,

Today I wish to laugh more and take this day easy. What may I do to lighten my load and walk with a lighter step?

Perhaps today I will try something new, do something fun, and laugh at myself when I take something too seriously.

The funniest moments of my life that I can

remember are _____,

_____, and _____.

Whenever I start to feel down or anxious, may I remember these lighthearted times and be filled with that joy once again.

Amen.

Unplugging

Dear God,

I have a lot on my plate. I am thankful that I have a few minutes with you this morning to be still and get my priorities for the day in line.

I have days when I feel like I am a hamster on a wheel. Today's modern devices keep me "connected," but sometimes I feel *too* connected. I multitask rather than get anything important accomplished. My best hours of the day can be squandered on mindless activities, such as checking e-mail and social media or watching too much television.

I can try to take frequent breaks from my desk and allow only certain times in my day to check my phone or be on my computer. I can choose to turn on the television only when a program is on that I actually wish to watch. I can read, write, take a walk, or just pray and be with you. The silence is nice. May my mind and body follow your lead for a moment and be still.

When I start to feel too connected and overwhelmed, may I remember that my most important connection is with you.

Amen.

Beautiful Morning

Dear God,.

Thank you for this beautiful morning. I appreciate the little things

that make my life so rich, such as _____,

_____, and _____.

I am loved, and I am at peace. I know that this is going to be a
wonderful day!

Amen.

My Goal for Today

Dear God,

The house is still quiet, and the sun's light is just beginning to flicker
into the room. I slept well, and I look forward to what this day may
bring. Today I am setting a goal to take some time to rest, to spend
time outdoors, and to be creative.

Amen.

Lessons

Dear God,

This morning I reflect on the many lessons you have taught me.

A few of the important lessons I have learned are:

1. _____

2._____

3._____

I still need help with this one, which I never seem to get

right: _____.

What more would you like me to know? What lessons from the past no longer serve me? Which newer lessons are the really important ones?

I know that there are no mistakes. As long as I am learning, I continue to grow.

Amen.

A Higher Purpose

Dear God,

What should I do with this day? When I feel aimless and scattered, please guide me to a higher purpose.

Perhaps I will sit and be still with you awhile... in the silence I will listen. I will breathe. I am confident clarity is close at hand.

Amen.

This, Too, Shall Pass

Dear God,

I have been under some stress lately, and I pray for peace. Please give me the strength and wisdom to get through this trying chapter.

If I felt sad, hurt, or weak, what would you say to me? When I get silent and breathe deeply... I know the answer.

Thank you. I am strong. This, too, shall pass.

Amen.

Close Calls

Dear God,

There have been close calls in my life, such as nearly being in a car accident, health scares,

and _____.

After these events happen, I am always greatly relieved and reminded how precious each day really is. I take nothing for granted, and I am grateful for this day and any other days I am blessed enough to experience.

Thank you for this sweet life. May I remain present and not squander this precious day.

Amen.

On Being Myself

Dear God,

Sometimes I am tempted to be something and someone I am not. I aim to impress, and I worry about stumbling in the eyes and opinions of others. When I find my center and pray with you, I realize that what I am doing is causing unnecessary stress on myself. Instead, I should be focusing my attention on better aspirations.

With your help, may I stand tall and confident knowing it is fine to just be myself. In fact, it is better than fine. When I doubt myself, please let me see the beautiful person you created when I look in the mirror. This world needs the real me with all my talents, skills, and quirks.

Amen.

Sharing My Light

Dear God,

I will do my best today to shine. May my smile uplift another who feels sad. May I be bold and do something that is challenging for me. By stretching and taking a step out of my comfort zone, may I inspire others to do the same.

When we challenge ourselves, we discover courage and confidence, which we can then pass on to others.

What a brilliant way to live! May I be a shining example to younger people who are just starting to find their way in the world and to others who for whatever reason feel stuck.

When timidity tempts and I begin to chicken out, may I be reminded to not be afraid to shine... for someone out there may need my light.

Amen.

I Hear You

Dear God,

I hear you in the silence.

I hear you in the sounds of nature.

I hear you when
someone special in my life
tells me they love me
and when I hear a friend's
wonderful laughter.

Thank you for speaking to me
in so many ways and
listening to my prayers.

Amen.

About the Author

Debra DiPietro is a wife, mother, social media specialist, and award winning blogger. She holds degrees in communication, education, and law. Debra's passion and life purpose is to inspire others with her words, which she does in part  through her blog, *The Warm Milk Journal*. The mission of her blog—and what she wishes for herself and all her readers—is to help us live the life of our dreams by day and sleep restfully at night.

When she is not writing, you may find Debra walking on the beach near her home in Jacksonville, Florida, sweating it out at her local Bikram yoga studio, or planning her next great adventure with her husband, John.